Hustle Under Pressure

Awaken the Hustle in You to Survive Uncertain Times

MARIAN CLAVILLE BURKS

Hustle Under Pressure

Copyright © 2020 by Marian Claville Burks

All rights reserved. This book or any portion thereof may not be reproduced or used in any manner whatsoever without the express written permission of the publisher except for the use of brief quotations in a book review.

Printed in the United States of America

First Printing, 2020

ISBN 9798639366659

Hustle Under Pressure

This book is dedicated to my city, Shreveport, Louisiana. We have it in us to effect the change we want to see. Let's make the world a believer. I love you, Shreveport!

CONTENTS

Foreward:	i
Introduction:	iii
Preface:	ix
Chapter 1: What is a Hustler?	2
Chapter 2: Pitfalls and Myths	25
Chapter 3: That's Law!	40
Chapter 4: Go and Hustle!	50
Chapter 5: 111 Ways	52
About The Author:	86

Hustle Under Pressure

Foreword

How many times have I, or even you, experienced a hardship in life, that not only left you broken but left you BROKE! I can't count how many times life has thrown me a blow and it took me extended time to recover, not only physically but financially. On the other hand, have you ever encountered this certain type of person that no matter how hard of a blow life threw, no matter how hard they fall, they seem to ALWAYS bounce back and land dead on their feet! Not only do they land on their feet, they use what knocked them down as part of their come up. You begin to wonder what is it about them that makes them so resilient, so strong, or even so special? What do they have or know that you don't? Is there something different that they are doing that you're not which allows them to always come out on top? I can say, I've thought these things countless times as I've watched Marian turn struggle into hustle and made gold out of rocks! There's a very unique brilliance and street-savvy that Marian has that's unparalleled by any other. When I think of her, I see the definition of a bona fide hustler. I've witnessed her grind relentlessly to get what she needs and then some. In Hustle Under Pressure, Marian not only shares her real-life trials and triumphs, she also breaks down the anatomy of a true hustler and the laws that govern such. As you read this book, you will laugh, you may even cry, but most importantly, you will be challenged and awakened to the hustler that lives inside of you! As you read, you will see how Marian has poured her entire self into this book and left everything on the table you need to awaken the hustler in you. Not only that, she gives you 111 ways to hustle NOW! As the true hustler she is, she leaves you without any excuse to survive and thrive, even in uncertain times. May the hustler in you come alive and thrive!

Ebony A. Harris
Founder, The Empowered Life Institute

Introduction

When you must write, the task itself can be difficult. You want to get your point across so badly, but you freeze up. You have so many great thoughts and ideas flowing through your mind, but when it comes time to write, it's like, *Duh, what should I say?* I am hoping the thoughts in my mind regarding the hustle a person must have not only to survive, but to thrive, will flow freely from my mind to yours.

Why do I feel the need to write a hustler's guide? Put simply, my city needs it. I grew up right here in Shreveport, Louisiana, and I have seen a lot of things. I have seen it all. I have seen well-meaning mothers resort to stealing clothes, food, and medicine. I have seen the same well-meaning women try to "game" the system that gamed them in the first place. I have seen food stamp fraud and money laundering. I have seen drugs - lots of drugs - being sold in order to put food on the table. I've then seen the same drugs used by the seller because there *is* no food to eat. I have seen brothers break into stores then have mothers go back to those *same* stores to cash in the coins that were stolen.

I have seen teenage boys get on Greyhound buses with suitcases filled with God knows what, working deals for men who could have easily been their fathers. Those boys needed to feel a father's love. Of course, they got very little money from the deals, but they somehow felt a connection to those older men. I have seen otherwise smart girls sell their bodies for what they thought was love and affection, but ultimately, it was for financial gain. Even though we are raised to think that money is the root of all evil, it seems like being *without* money brings on all sorts of evil.

I am draped in the DNA of a hustler. I didn't know my father well, but I've been told that my hustle comes from him. I have always had a fascination with making money. That fascination only increased because during my childhood, we did not have any. To say that we were poor would be an understatement. Eight of us - my grandmother, mother, three brothers, two uncles, and I - lived in a 2-bedroom, 1-bath home on a dead-end street. Relatives were always [temporarily] staying with us. We had our issues and a whole lot of roaches, but we also had love. I was not fully aware of how poor we really were, but I could feel the affects all around me.

One of my brothers was what you could consider a "professional" thief. My mother was proud of us no matter what we did, and she continues to be today. She did the best she could with us and would say, with a big grin followed by squeaky laugh, "Andy can steal sweet out of sugar!" He would steal anything from cars to bikes and break in any place from homes to grocery stores. He was very good at it. He used to steal pizzas to feed us. We loved those days because we rarely had pizza.

One of my uncles would clean offices in the mornings and sell crack on the weekends. He also loved to cook so whatever money he made from selling crack went first to his habits, then to our food supply. My mom worked overnight and during the day, so she was never home. Her money went toward the mortgage, lights, gas, and things like that. She would not put all our daddies on child support because, in her own words, she did not want to "inconvenience them". *Sheesh!* She finally put my father on child support, though, because he did not want to claim me.

My grandmother kept up with us the best way she could in the late 80s "hood". She was our churchgoing, calm-spirited, intelligent, family guidepost---she was our rock. I am so thankful that she raised me and am proud to have inherited her demeanor. She told the truth and did not seem to be afraid of anything. It was like she had magic. But all the magic in all the world could not relieve the stress and strain that came with being black and broke in a place like Shreveport.

Shreveport is the third largest city in the state of Louisiana. Dr. Martin Luther King Jr. called it the most racist city he had ever been in. Now that's saying something. Coupled with being broke, being black during the Jim Crow era could be kind of depressing. While all this was going on around me -- all the poverty, drugs, theft, and so much more -- I managed to remain optimistic. I often daydreamed and fantasized about a better life because if I had focused on the circumstances at-hand, I would not have made it out of what some saw as a vicious cycle. My mind and body defended themselves from reality with fantasy and imagination.

I had a firm belief that if I could find the gold at the end of the rainbow, everything would be alright. I loved watching those 80s movies that showed kids going on wild adventures and, in the end, finding the pot of gold! I was determined to find my own pot of gold! At six years old, I went looking for that pot of gold in my backyard when one of my uncles shouted from the backdoor, "Ain't no damn gold back here! That shit just in the movies" with his Kool cigarette hanging from his lip. I quickly shot back with, "Fuck you! When I find it, you can't get none!" The man I had learned those cuss words from just laughed, waved his hand, and disappeared into the house in a puff of cigarette smoke. I dug and dug and dug but didn't find any gold. I came in the house sad, crying, and feeling dejected.

My grandmother had recently passed away and since my mother was working double shifts, my brothers often had to "keep me". My brother, who was four years my senior, and I were alone most times. I spent lots of time thinking about ways to make money to save my family. Then one day it hit me. Eureka! I would sell lemonade! It worked for the white kids I saw on TV, so it had to work for me, right?

I went into the kitchen, got out a Kool-Aid pitcher, some lemon juice, a ***whole*** bag of sugar, some tap water, and whipped up a batch. My brother just looked at me and shook his head as I put a table and chair at the edge of our yard. Over the years, my family had collected a large assortment of plastic cups from businesses all over the city so I gathered as many as I could and put them on my "lemonade stand". I carefully brought out my pitcher of lemonade which really wasn't much more than sugar, tap water, and the essence of lemon.

Finally, I sat down at the table that proudly displayed the sign I made which read "Lemonade $0.50" and waited for the money to roll in. I waited, waited, and waited…no customers. Remember earlier, I mentioned that I lived on a dead-end street. Well, that day, I learned my first business lesson and that is that location is everything! Location, location, location! Just as tears started to well up in my eyes, a neighbor from across the street who had been raking his yard came over, gave me $0.50, and asked for a cup of lemonade!

I was so happy to have a customer, I spilled his first cup! Although I know he really didn't want to drink that sugar water with the mysterious black specs floating around in it, I could tell he had respect for my efforts. His respect for my efforts led me to learn the second hustler lesson at a young age: show up and perform the act the best you can whether it's for one person or a million people.

Even though I had a harder childhood than some, I don't want anyone to feel bad for me. I am grateful for everything that happened in my life. I have never failed. I have always learned. The purpose of this book is to help the people of my city and the world see that even if they come from a place similar to the one I came from, they don't have to stay there. If you apply these hustler lessons and skills, you will be better for it.

Money is literally made from trees, so there is more than enough for all of us. We don't have to hate on each other or try to knock the next man or woman down to get what we want. If we all win, *we all win*. If you follow the lessons in this guide, not only will you win, you will thrive wherever you are in the world. Forget New York – hell, if you can make it *here*, you can literally be dropped anywhere on Earth and make it happen. Make this year the last year that you struggle. Let's get it!

Preface

It is my hope that this book acts as a guide for the people in the city I love and to those in cities like it all over the world. Jim Crow has beaten us down, racism has beaten us down, low-level education has beaten us down. Gang violence, drugs, low self-esteem, low self-efficacy, and as of late, COVID-19, has crippled us, but there is a way around this. You can thrive here or anywhere with a shift in your mindset and by learning that there is opportunity where others see obstacles. This hustle guide will help you see things differently. I will recount for you how I came to learn the lessons I share throughout the book. I will breakdown the hustler's laws and pitfalls. My hope and prayer are that you will utilize some or all the recommendations in this guide to move from merely surviving to thriving. I come from where you come from. Once you learn the hustle and began to thrive, reach back and help the next person win. We can change a whole generation. I know there's a fighter inside you - you got this! Let's show the world what we are made of and make them believers. I love you.

Hustle Under Pressure

Chapter 1: What is a Hustler?

> "We represent a hustler. I think we represent inspiration. I think we represent, you know, staying down. I think we represent building yourself up from the bootstraps."
> -Nipsey Hussle

Genetically, your DNA has memory. In an article published on April 27, 2018, on Science Alert's website (www.sciencealert.com), Signe Dean wrote, "The most important set of genetic instructions we all get comes from our DNA, passed down through generations. But the environment we live in can make genetic changes, too."

The art of hustle comes largely from our environment. We decide early on whether we will sink or swim, eat or starve, live or die. Some of us are born with a genetic inheritance. I did not have a relationship with my father. My loving mother would say things like, "You hustle like your daddy." She told me stories about how he opened convenience stores, sold drugs, and pimped women. She would say, "He always had his hand in something just like you." It was like I couldn't help but want to "hit a lick" or get capital gains from my endeavors. It is a part of my DNA.

My mother's brothers had it, too. They were always starting companies, buying real estate, and working what we deemed as good jobs. I was always fascinated with making money, especially since I started with nothing. It became a game to me. How much money could I collect? What could I do to make more money? What exactly would people pay for?

After my lemonade stand misadventure, I moved on to other ventures. I stole newspapers out of different neighbor's yards and sold them to other neighbors. I found out that was illegal. Okay, I knew it was illegal all along, but now that others knew what I was doing, I stopped. I would have my mom put a $1.00 bill in the newspaper machine then I would grab all the newspapers out. After that, I would go where I knew a crowd of people would be and sell the papers. I stopped doing that when I was run off by the homeless men who were doing the same thing.

Soon after that, I started bagging groceries when my mom would go to the grocery store. I figured that while she was shopping, I would make some extra money bagging people's groceries. I saw the neighborhood boys doing it all the time and I knew I was faster and more organized than they were. I damn sure knew not to put the can goods on top of the eggs like those dummies did. After I would sack the people's groceries, they would just say "thank you" without paying me any money. Finally, after this happened with the 10th family, I asked why they didn't pay me like they paid the others. I was told it was because I was a girl. "Girls don't sack groceries." That was my first encounter with sexism on the job. I said fuck that, and I quit. Side note here: my mom is the bomb.com! She would just let me do me and would stay in the background supporting me. She didn't quite understand my ambitions, but she knew I had to be me. I love her deeply for that.

The Birth of a Hustler

Out of necessity, hustlers are born. I believe if we had been provided with everything at birth, we would not hustle as hard as we do. I ask myself all the time if I had had a stable family-base, would I have started out a businesswoman instead of a hustler? Either way the hustle would have been in me, but I wonder at what capacity. Since hustle is strengthened out of necessity, I remember a few occasions when my hustle was solidified.

The first incident happened when I was about seven years old. My mother had 4 children, with three different fathers. My brother, Don, and I have the same father. We are the last two of the bunch and I am the youngest. I remember my mother called my father and asked if he would send money for us to eat. I was lying on her stomach with hunger pangs and I could hear my father on the other end of our mustard yellow corded phone telling my mother, "Have them eat air pudding." My mother looked me in my eyes, laughed a little, said, "Okay" into the mouthpiece then hung up the phone. I asked my mother what air pudding was. With a disappointed grin, she told me that air pudding meant "nothing". I swallowed hard and made an internal promise that my mother would not have to make that call again and that I would not depend on another soul to eat.

Another time my hustle was solidified was when I found myself in "full-hustle" mode when I had a summer job through the City of Shreveport youth job program. I was 14 and had another job downtown and it happened to be just up the street from my first job. I would work my first job and on my lunch break, I would walk to the job downtown, then go back to the other.

My mom didn't have a car, so I had to catch the bus. One day, my uncle Billy saw me walking to the bus stop, stopped me, and told me to get in. My Uncle Billy was known as the "rich uncle". My family labeled him as money hungry and stingy, but I always loved his spirit. He had started a childcare center and had lots of real estate. My family and other people would always ask him for money.

My pride had grown strong and hard by then and I promised myself I would never ask him or anyone else for anything. That day in his car, when he asked me where I was going, I told him to catch the bus home. He asked what I was doing downtown, and I told him I had been working my jobs. He smirked. He pulled up at my house (which he happened to own) and I thanked him. Before I got out, he said, "Shanna here you go". He handed me $20. I said, "No, I'm good." He said, "Take the money." There was no pity in his eyes, only great pride. I took the money and I stuck my chest out because I knew that a true hustler had recognized a true hustler. I was born and matured in my hustle because of my mindset.

Mindset

Whether or not you were born a hustler, there are some mindsets that must be adopted or you will lose at the hustle game..

Let me clarify that a hustler's mindset is different from a businessperson's mindset. A hustler *must* get it by any means. It's their way to eat and live. A hustler may not have everything in place to succeed, but they sure know how to get it done. A businessperson knows *how* to work what he or she has been provided with. The businessperson's mindset is strategic, calculated, and purposeful. A businessperson may have the necessary tools in place and know how to create a structed plan to build upon. Both mindsets can be one in the same, however, the business mindset elevates you to another level. This guide will focus on the mindset of a hustler. Here are the mindsets you must adopt to be a true hustler:

Don't Be Negative

"Positive thinking will let you do everything better than negative thinking will." - Zig Ziglar

"A man is but the product of his thoughts. What he thinks, he becomes."
– Mahatma Gandhi, Indian leader

In difficult times, trying times, loving times, happy times - anytime - negative thinking will steal all joy. For a hustler, any form of negative thinking will kill your deal. Negative thinking affects your energy. To be at the top of your hustle, people must be drawn to you and no one likes to be around a negative person. Negative people are like that rain cloud that follows cartoon characters around on a bad day. Those types of people are social terrorists. They look for opportunities to prey on people's shortcomings and fears. Their favorite sayings include things like, "Yeah, but…", "Yeah, that sounds good, but that won't work", "Yeah, but, that's too good to be true.", "Yeah, but that virus will kill you." Blah, blah, blah.

Here is a quick test to take to see if you are negative as hell.
https://www.mindtools.com/pages/article/newTCS_89.htm

This test will give you great perspective. I scored right in the middle so I still have work to do and I am aware of what I need to do.

Here are some things you can do to assure that you don't become negative or to stop being negative:

- Watch the words you speak. Take words like can't, try, need, and want out of your vocabulary and replace them with can, will, have, and desire.
- Train your thoughts. When you start thinking negative things, switch your thoughts. It's that simple, but to help you train your brain wear a rubber band on your wrist. Whenever you think something negative or speak something negative, pop yourself with the rubber band. After a while you will stop having negative thoughts.
- Watch positive YouTube videos. There are so many inspirational videos available. Subscribe to those videos and watch them daily. Watch them as soon as you wake up in the morning, before getting on Facebook, and right before you go to sleep at night so you will have positive vibes deep in your subconscious. Here are some of my favorite YouTube channels for inspiration:
    o [Rev. Ike](#)
    o [Patrice Washington](#)
    o [Bob Proctor](#)
    o [Inspiring Habit](#)

- Listen to positive, upbeat music that lifts your energy and makes you move - Stevie Wonder, Joelle Monee, Michael Jackson, Jill Scott - just to name a few.
- Laugh a lot!! Scientifically, it is proven that the more you laugh the better your overall energy level will be and the more positive you will be.

Hustling can sometimes suck the optimism out of you. You must take the time to keep yourself in check and stay positive.

Problems are Opportunities

"Everything negative - pressure, challenges - is all an opportunity for me to rise."
- Kobe Bryant

What keeps the poor "poor", is seeing problems instead of opportunity. It's seeing the glass as half-empty or focusing on someone else's glass instead of making yours do what it does. Life is not fair, but we all have an opportunity to play the hand we are dealt the best way we can. Thank God it's 2020, and information is just at your fingertips. We walk around with super computers in our pockets and we can learn just about anything online.

I remember back in the early 90s when the internet was new and to get the bulk of your information or to be able to use a computer with access to the internet, you had to go to the library. I have always loved everything about information! There's no better high for me than to consume information and learn something new. My mom, on the other hand, was less than thrilled with my fasciation. She supported whatever I wanted to do, but she said, "You are the only child I know that I have to beat to leave the library!" She would drive me to the downtown library since it was open on Sundays and had more information than the neighborhood libraries. She would walk me in then sit at one of the wooden tables on the first floor amongst the other tired moms and dads and the Shreveport homeless population. I felt right at home staring at that computer screen!

On one of our visits downtown, we were stopped by the police a few yards from the library. The police officer asked my mom if she knew that her vehicle had been identified in a rash of gasoline thefts and asked if she had a husband or sons. My mom, as cool and sweet as possible, said, "No, sir, I just purchased this van." He looked at her for what seemed like forever and said, "Okay." He then told her he would take those notes out of the system and told us to have a nice day. As the police officer drove off, she looked over at me and said, "I'm going to kick your brother Don's ass when I get home!" He had been the one stealing gas in her van. "And I should turn this mutherfucker around and go straight home! You better make this trip damn worth it!" Knowing that my mom rarely got upset, I was determined to make this trip worth it.

I got on the only available computer on the first floor and searched "how to make money in middle school". The AOL man ran across the screen at a snail's pace compared to today's high-speed internet connections. Once it did load, I read a few articles about some white kids making things and selling them for a school project. Blah blah blah.

Then I came across an article about a black girl who made cookies and sold them at school. Other people were selling stuff at her school, but what made her product different was her packaging. I didn't know how to bake, but it spurred an idea. I asked my mom if she had any more food stamps left and she said she had a few. I asked her to take me to County Market. Once there, I looked for something – anything - different that was not being sold at school. We had kids who made Kool-Aid bags and others were selling candy bars. I knew I had to be different and I had to make it make sense money-wise. I looked and looked, then I found them!! Green caramel candy apple suckers!

I purchased two bags of 25 suckers for $2.50 per bag and I sold each sucker for $0.50 per sucker. I would re-up three times a week. At the height of my venture, I was making $75 per week! I had a business strategy that worked. I would not try to sell to everybody, I would sell strictly to the kids of the Bottom Boys! The Bottom Boys were a well-known gang and had the most organized crime game in the area. Many of them had been arrested and some of their kids were considered to be "hood rich". They had the initialed herringbone necklaces and rings, and all the latest Jordans and Tommy Hilfiger. They had gold teeth and tattoos in middle school and ninth grade! I remember one of my best customers, Quita, would stay fresh in Tommy and Jordans. I swear it looked like she shinned her gold tooth just to shine on everyone.

I ran it to Quita like this, "Hey friend, you know no one else has these suckers. Nobody even knows they exist, and they are soooooo good! You can buy a whole bag and have a new sucker in your mouth all day! Hell, everybody got them raggedy ass candy bars and you can stick these suckers in your ponytail and pull them out all day!" I had her at ponytail! I made a big show of her giving me so much money then I would make a sign that said, "SOLD OUT CATCH ME TOMORROW!" and staple it to my purse!! Her gold tooth beamed knowing that she had cleaned me out! I would come home with the money and help my mom buy groceries or something different than leg quarters to eat. Instead of looking at what we lacked, I always looked for opportunity.

Where is there a problem you can see in and around your life? If you recognize something as a problem, more than likely there is an opportunity to provide a solution. A lot of times, the solution can be monetized. What problem can you solve today that will make you more money?

Don't Give Up, Just Adjust

> "Don't give up before the miracle happens."
> – Fannie Flagg

I guess you can say I have an obsessive personality. I can take things to the extreme. When my daughter was born, I was so nervous about having people keep her that I did the only logical thing I knew to do. I started a childcare center. Logical, right?! I found a building, staffed it, got a feeding program, and a lot of kids. That's the super-short version. The more extended version is that I had to deal with my then-boyfriend, who is now my husband, telling me that I was crazy for leaving the post office where I was making $60K a year and that he did not support me. I had to deal with "friends" talking about me behind my back and saying slick shit like, "How your little business coming along?" or "How many kids are there now?" or "Oh, it must be nice". To stay sane, I would often say to them (in my head of course), "Bitch, shut the fuck up...no-vision-having-ass hoe!" Then I would laugh to myself and say to them, "Business is good!" On top of that, I was not making any money and my mom, who was working with me, was not making any money either even though she was doing the bulk of the work.

To be fair, my husband did not understand my madness, but he did pay all the bills while I explored myself and found what I wanted to do. With his financial support, I was able to find myself and for that, I am grateful. I digress. The daycare business grew fast, but I was not passionate about it. I started it to keep my daughter in an environment I knew was safe, however, it was financially and emotionally draining. It had gotten so bad, the daycare's lights were about to be cut off and my mom didn't have enough money to get her diabetes medicine. I was gaining weight and had raggedy looking clothes. Those "friends" were getting a real kick out of me looking like I was feeling which was bad. I remember crying to my friend, Tiya, who is a brilliant businessowner, telling her that I was a failure and that I should do what my boyfriend suggested which was go to nursing school or to get my master's in business. I remember Tiya, who has a master's degree in business, by the way, saying, "Marian, God did not bring you this far to leave you. This is not your finishing point. You just need to adjust."

Once she said that, it was like a lightbulb went off in my mind. I wiped my face, gave her a hug then got to work! I remembered that just a year prior, the daycare I now owned didn't even exist, so that was an accomplishment in itself and that I could write the story of my life the way *I* wanted to. I didn't have to settle for anyone else's version of *my* story. That same week, a local church reached out to me about helping them start a childcare center. They had gotten my information from the local childcare center network because they were amazed at how fast I started the center. The church paid me to consult for them and I sold them my business.

I researched work-from-homes jobs because I still wanted to be home with my baby and if I had to, I would just pay my mom to keep my baby. I found out about Nielsen TV ratings and became a membership rep with them. While working at Nielsen, I had the opportunity to learn about real estate investing and the business of real estate through a podcast on Biggerpocket's website. I learned about other money-making businesses I never knew existed through Pat Flynn's *Smart Passive Income* podcast and as they say, the rest is history. I became a real estate investor and a successful realtor. I also strategically help my clients open companies and pad their life through real estate investments. If I would have given up and not adjusted, I would be like the walking dead. I would have just let my dreams die. As a hustler, you will fail, but what matters is how you adjust. Adjust wherever needed, but NEVER give up.

Connect with Other Hustlers

"Locate things that motivate you and surround yourself with people that inspire you."
- Sunday Adelaja

"One of the greatest values of mentors is the ability to see ahead what others cannot see and to help them navigate a course to their destination." — John C. Maxwell

I have been very fortunate in my life to have had wonderful mentors who were and are ultimate hustlers in different ways. I am grateful for them allowing me to be in their presence because they didn't have to. A lot of people see the statement I just made as "kissing ass" and that's the difference between a winner and a failure. Failures think they can get somewhere by themselves while winners know to get anywhere faster, they need a road map of life experiences from those who have lived it before them. I have been blessed to be good friends with one of the top business consultants in Louisiana, Tiya Scroggins, and personally mentored by one of the top businessmen in Louisiana you will never know, Donald Horton. I have had mentors who were younger than I am, older than I am, different races from mine, different religions than mine, and even different sexual orientations than mine. One of the mentors that sticks out in my mind who I believe I learned the most from is a local DJ named Terrance Stewart. You would know him as BayBay.

BayBay is one of the funniest, most charismatic people I have ever met. We are cousins, but we were introduced as friends. I cannot explain how we became instant friends, but all I know is I *always* gravitate to the biggest hustler in the room. I just want to soak up everything I can learn. I never want anything from the relationship but to learn. Anyway, what I remember was my two best friends, Marquita and Tanikki, and I were selling "faux daiquiris" at a teen club called The Mansion. One night, it was slow, and BayBay was there. He was joking around with us as he was about to leave when I asked him if we could go with him to the next event. We went and had a great time! After the club adventure was over, he asked if we would come to his house with him. He just liked our energy.

We went back to his house and watched Tyler Perry's *Madea* plays all night and I cooked breakfast while we watched. After that day, I would go over just to be around him. I would watch him make copies of mixtape CDs and listen to his phone conversations with people like Daymond John of FUBU, Lil Flip, and DJ Khalid. He would also have me do things like drive him to warehouses to get more CDs, to his insurance provider to get rider insurance for his events, and to support local businesses. He would explain basic things to me like making sure I kept my car clean (I still struggle with this) because how I treat my things determines how much I will be blessed later. I remember watching him blow leaves out of all his neighbor's yards for free while he was doing his own yard. I asked him why he did that and he said because people will always remember how you made them feel even if they forget what you do. BayBay is a standup guy.

One day I asked him if he would invest in me and my friends throwing a party. He asked me what I knew about throwing parties. I jokingly told him I had watched him do it. He was not amused. He asked, "Seriously, what do you know?" I told him that the DJ would cost $500, the venue rental would be $800, and that I would split the cost with my two friends to pay him back if the party was a bust. If it was a success, though, which it would be, I would split the profits with them. I told him we would give him $1500 back on his $1300 investment. He told me before he gave me the money, I should really talk to my friends to see if they were all in and to really think about what goes into a successful party. I talked to my friends and came back to him and said we were all in. He said, "Okay, this is not as simple as it looks, but here is the money."

He gave me the $1300 and I went and paid the DJ's fee and the rental fee for the venue. We had some fliers made and went to the mall to pass them out. We were a week away from the event and things seemed to be going well. My friends were supportive, but they are natural introverts. They like who they like so it was a little more difficult inviting people that they didn't know or like. I was a relatively unknown person and the people who did know me didn't equate me with a fun time.

Hustle Under Pressure

Friday came absolutely NO ONE SHOWED UP! It was just me, my two friends, and the DJ. Sick is not a strong enough word to describe what I felt that night. We didn't make one red cent in profit and we were in the hole $500 each. I didn't know where we went wrong. The next morning BayBay called me and asked, "What's up? How did it go?" I said, "Terrible" but that we would have his money to him in a week. He laughed and said, "Okay cool. Once you give me my money, we need to talk."

The next week, we had scrapped up his money. He came and picked it up with one of his girlfriends in his burnt orange Aerostar van which was on gold Dayton spoke rims. He told me to come by his house the next morning for a lesson. I went the next morning with a million reasons why it didn't work: Shreveport is too small, the age group we were targeting had gone to off to college, my friends didn't help me enough, blah, blah, blah. When I started to tell him those things, he stopped pressing CDs and said the following:

"Nah, little sis, what it is, I know people like me make this look easy, but there is a science to this. Jabba Jaws (another local DJ legend) fronted me the money for promotion so getting fronted the money isn't a big deal, you just need to know what to do with it. Here is the what you should have done:

1. Partnered with someone out here that's been doing this. You could have asked me or other

Hustle Under Pressure

people out here who been doing it instead of trying to be the big dog on your own.
2. You haven't formed enough relationships in that area to be known for parties. People come to my parties because I show love to everybody. That didn't happen overnight...that takes time. You genuinely must care about people and get involved in their lives.
3. Your team is everything. Everyone must have the same goal and work towards it together.
4. If you fail keep going and learn from it. We have failed a lot, but we learn and keep it moving.
5. Master what you love to do. I don't know if you are in love with this or not, but whatever you love, dedicate yourself to it and study those who are successful and learn from them.

I know this is not how you wanted it to turn out, but I am proud of you for trying it."

After that talk, I really knew that there was more to him than just being a DJ. I was in the presence of a high-level businessman and I was grateful. I learned a lot from him while we were close. I learned things no business school could ever teach.

Who do you look up to? I would say do whatever you can to be in their presence because the knowledge you get from them will never fade away.

Be Excellent in All Things You Do

"We are what we repeatedly do. Excellence, then, is not an act, but a habit."

-Aristotle

Excellence can be an intimidating word. When you think of excellence, most likely, you think of perfection. Really, though, excellence is doing the very best you can do, day after day after day, even when you don't feel like it. My real-life example of excellence is my husband. My husband is what I call a "calculated hustler". I am all creative and mostly reactionary. My husband is proactive and methodical in his actions, especially when it comes to money and life. My husband is a truck driver and when I met him, he was a driving trainer for Swift Transportation. He currently drops gasoline for Dupree Logistics, where he is the top-ranked driver in the company. When my husband met me, I was working at the food stamp office as a caseworker and I was selling bootleg purses on the side. When I took my then-boyfriend to meet my purse plug, he immediately saw I was losing money to the plug and called him out on it. The plug was upset, but I knew I had found my mate.

He efficiently and consistently made proactive moves that made his credit excellent, his retirement fund completely maxed, and our household more than comfortable. My husband makes sure he turns all his money the same way in his wallet and doesn't believe in being wasteful. We are never less than first-class anywhere we go. His vehicles, shoes, clothes, and hair cut stays clean, crisp, and excellent. He is not perfect, yet he is excellent in everything he does. I have learned the value of being excellent and the best I can be in everything I do. It may seem mundane, however, in my husband's words, "If you not playing to win, what are you playing for?"

Hustlers are not perfect, but we find a level of excellence and play there consistently. Where do you need to be excellent at?

Know Yourself

"The privilege of a lifetime is to become who you truly are."
– Carl Jung

"Knowing yourself is the beginning of all wisdom."
– Aristotle

"Honesty and transparency make you vulnerable. Be honest and transparent anyway."
- Mother Theresa

I have always been different from most of my peers. Even when I tried hard to fit in and think like the group, I never could. Even when I tried to think like my family, I just couldn't. What caused a lot of issues is not only could I not think like the collective, I could not shut up about how I felt either. People would say things like, "Marian you sure don't mind being extra open and vulnerable." The secret is, I really don't know how to be. It takes too much brain power for me to hold back so I might as well just be me. I am sentimental, a go-getter, passionate, motivating, smart, seductive, funny, friendly, and free. I have started so many companies and had so many jobs. I hopped from job to job and project to project until I found my life's purpose.

My life's purpose is to empower, encourage, educate, and motivate people, especially black people, to create generational wealth, become financially independent, grow companies/business of excellence, and to realize their full potentials in life. I must be a shining example of my mission so that I can help other people get there. Y'all, life is super short and you will be super pissed if you get to the end of it and didn't get to know yourself and live your most authentic life. One of the books that helped me find my purpose was *The ONE Thing* by Gary W. Keller and Jay Papasan. This book and the activities inside it helped me narrow down who I really am. I have taken numerous personal assessments like Myers Briggs test, the four-color personality test, Keller Personality Assessment, and spiritual gift assessments.

I spend time with myself often. I fast and pray for wisdom and insight. I do what feels right for me even when it feels uncomfortable. I challenge myself often and do new things because in doing new things, it teaches you who you are. I mediate in the morning and at night. I admire and enjoy myself. There is freedom in knowing who you are. Every true hustler must know where they are in life, where they can bend, and they should damn sure know where to draw the line in the sand. Get to know and love yourself. You will not regret it.

Being born a hustler doesn't always mean you will be successful. You must adopt the mindset of a hustler by not being negative; seeing opportunities, not problems; not giving up, just adjusting; connecting with other hustlers; being excellent; and knowing yourself. Even with these tools of mindset in play, you must avoid, at all costs, the pitfalls and myths all hustlers encounter in their lives.

Chapter 2: Pitfalls and Myths

Hustlers are a unique breed of people. We may own our own businesses, or we may be at the top of our fields or corporate jobs. Our hustle is unmatched and often challenged. We are challenged by the pitfalls of the environment, by relationships, by poor spending habits, by "shiny object syndrome", and by being overly generous. We must also combat the lies that society tries to shackle us down with that we will talk about later in this chapter. Let's explore these pitfalls first. Once you recognize them, do your best to eliminate them or adjust them to your advantage.

Pitfalls

1. Environments

"You are a product of your environment. So, choose the environment that will best develop you toward your objective. Analyze your life in terms of its environment. Are the things around you helping you toward success - or are they holding you back?"
-W. Clement Stone

Some environments naturally help you to thrive while others seem like their main objective is to kill you. We all have choices. The power to choose can be a life altering event. Most people don't really see their environment as helping or hurting them because it is all they know, and they have never experienced contrast. You must take some time and truly observe your surroundings. Ask yourself if your environment is conducive to growth. Can I live my greatest life here? If the answer is no, the simple thing to do is change it. I have a good friend and business colleague who is from the very small town called Many, Louisiana. In most small towns there are not very many economic opportunities.

No opportunity is typically the pre-cursor for poverty, addiction, imprisonment, and teen pregnancy. However, my friend has always wanted more for his life. Although he hungered for bigger goals, bigger dreams and something completely different, he loves his hometown. It has provided the roots of his hustle and the spirit of the people is forever encouraging. Nonetheless he did not completely escape the negative aspects that sometimes come along with growing up poor. As a teenager he was arrested several times, most times it was just police harassment. There were times when he experienced violence, one incident of gunplay lead to his cousin being shot while he was standing a few feet away.

He was encouraged by his mother and other friends from his neighborhood to join the military. During the initial stages of his military career, he struggled to conform and did not totally respect authority. As he matured and experienced life, he changed his actions and eventually retired from the Air Force with honors. He left the military to become an entrepreneur developing two different businesses within 5 years. He is now the sole proprietor of Palmer Industrial, a Real Estate development and construction company, serving the regional area of north Louisiana.

Justin Palmer often says, "Exposure is important for growth and progress. I was lucky enough to be exposed to different ways of life at a young age. My childhood in Many gave me something that cannot be taught in a classroom." In his hometown Justin learned that if you choose to rise, the environment has already prepared you to succeed.

You can't help where you are born, but you can change the way you utilize and see your environment. Read different books, watch different shows, listen to different YouTube videos and music. Change the environment of your spirit first and then the physical environment will follow.

2. Wrong Relationships

> "Losing excess fats through exercise is important, but losing useless friends is urgent. Treat urgent things first!"
> ― Israelmore Ayivor,
> Let's go to the Next Level

Whew, chile! I could literally write a book, *a whole series of books*, on this topic. My transparent moment: I am in need of love and I sometimes get it from wherever I can, even if it's the wrong place. Thank God I know that about myself, so when it is time for me to break free, it's not difficult for me. What does wrong relationships have to do with how you hustle? EVERYTHING! Having the wrong friends, family members in your space, or the wrong mate will knock you off your hustle game every time. In the movie *American Gangster*, Denzel Washington plays Harlem drug dealer, Frank Lucas. Even though Frank was immoral and ruthless, he had a system. Nothing too flashy, just systematic. He was a faceless, highly organized crime boss until his girlfriend, Eva, encouraged him to be flashy and wear a fur coat to an event. Had he listened to his own instincts, he would have not gotten on the investigator's radar and would have stayed on his merry way.

For me, I have dated men who didn't care about me, they just cared about what I could bring to the relationship. I have also had "friends" who cut me out of deals for as little as $2000 when I made sure they made $40K+. I have had family members that I love dearly not pay me what they owe me, cut me out of deals, and were down right discouraging on my ventures. I could tell you stories that would make you cry big crocodile tears about how much hurt I have experienced in the name of love, but I will not give those things a platform or any more energy because they are not worth it. Trust your instincts. You know when a relationship is giving you life or if it's draining the life out of you. If you don't here are a few quick questions to ask yourself about any relationship that will get you right:

- When I am in hustle mode, do they support me or do they distract me?
- Do they accuse me of not showing them enough attention when hustling must be done?
- Do they hustle with me or against me?
- Do they offer support the best way they can?
- Am I required to give them things just so they will show me love?

If any of these questions make you feel uncomfortable, it may be a sign that the relationship is not serving you. To be truly locked into your hustle, sometimes you must go it alone or allow the people who truly love you to show support the best way they know how. Shed the dead relationships by distancing yourself and become your own biggest fan. You don't want to comprise the value of your hustle for unhealthy relationships.

3. Excessive spending

"Don't tell me where your priorities are. Show me where you spend your money and I'll tell you what they are."
—James W. Frick

There was a time when I would spend ALL my money as soon as I got it! I remember telling myself when I hit a six-figure income, there would be no way I could spend it all. I call BS because I spent every bit of it! I went on trips, paid for our wedding, all in cash. We basically had three weddings. My favorite rapper, Bun B, was at one of our wedding celebrations. Y'all, a rapper! SMH! My mind-set as a hustler was, if I made that money once, I would make it again, and I did, however, my expenses exceeded my income. The formula for wealth goes like this: income − expenses = wealth. If your income is $200K and your expenses is $210K, your net worth is -$10k, which is bad. When you are hustling, especially if you come from a place where you didn't have money, it is easy to fall into the trap of spending all you have. If it was not for the savings habits of my excellent husband, I would be up shit creek. In times like this COVID-19 epidemic, it is important to save no less than six months to a year's worth of living expenses by any means necessary. Look at saving like a bill that must be paid or like tithing. Also educate yourself on making wise money choices with proven money leaders like Dave Ramsey, Talaat & Tai McNeely of the His & Her Money Podcast, BiggerPockets Money podcast, and The Budgetnista Tiffany Aliche. They will help you whip your budgets in shape. If nothing else, save $0.10 from every dollar you earn in online accounts like Ally or with stock purchasing apps like Robinhood or Acorns. While you are on your hustle, make sure you put something back for days like today, no matter what.

4. Overlooking details

> "The difference between something good and something great is attention to detail."
> – Charles R Swindoll, Pastor & Author

As a hustler, I am always on the go. The thrill of the deal gives me so much life that sometimes I overlook the details. For example, I am so excited to share this book so I can help people get from under financial stress that I know all too well, I am tempted to shave off some details. Knowing that about myself I enlisted the help of Ebony Allen Harris, who wrote the foreword, and my editor Trease Shine Hinton. I have watched these women over the years in business and in their personal lives and I admire their attention to detail and excellence in everything that they do. Ebony is a trained chef, dancer, pastor, teacher, and writer. What amazes me about her is that she is so powerful that she can literally do anything that she focuses on with superior excellence and precision. I have seen her put together entire productions with over 20 people to perfection.

Don't get so busy that you forget to take time to take care of yourself physically and emotionally.

Don't forget to spend time with your spouse and your kids. Take time to look at your money every week (i.e. balance your accounts), plan for every penny, and read financial books like The Richest Man in Babylon or my favorite The One Minute Millionaire. Before you commit to a project or anything, always say you must think about it first, even if it is just for 30 minutes. Take the time to count the cost of everything you do. You will never regret it.

5. Not mastering anything

"You must immerse yourself in your work. You must fall in love with your work ... You must dedicate your life to mastering your skill. That's the secret of success."
- Chef Jiro

"A jack of all trades is a master of none, but oftentimes better than a master of one."
-Robert Greene

As a hustler you must learn how to do a multitude of things, but if you don't take the time to master *something*, you will always be spinning your wheels. I am not saying to stop doing multiple things because that's necessary in times like these; however, when you master a skill, that skill will open opportunities for you that you have never had before. One of my real estate clients that I admire the most for his mastery is Mr. Shawn Boston. Mr.

Boston is literally a master barber. He takes grooming to a whole other level. Throughout his barbering career, he has opened a successful barbering school in two cities, has multiple locations, wins awards at hair shows across the country, and educates & uplifts his community with classes on brand management, getting assets, and much more. He is our city's male version of Madam CJ Walker in the flesh. He is all that and more because he decided to master the art of barbering.

Whatever it is that you are passionate about, master that one thing and let it open doors for you.

6. Covering up insecurities with welfare and generosity

"No more martyring myself."
– Sharon E. Rainey

"The only person who can pull me down is myself, and I'm not going to let myself pull me down anymore."
-C. JoyBell

We know the benefit of helping others, but we never look at the benefit of taking care of ourselves. We know it's better to give than to receive but receiving isn't bad either. I'm going to address the elephant in the room: *Black women are the worst at taking care of ourselves and we are public enemy #1 when it comes to covering up our insecurities and shortcomings with taking care of other people.* Sis, stop that shit! I'm talking to myself, too. Our spirits are solidified - you are not going to hell for taking care of yourself first. You will hustle all your life just to end up out of shape, alone, grumpy, and playing the victim. Hustle with the end in mind. Manifest the life you want because you are powerful enough to choose the exact life you want. You don't have to feel guilty for taking time to yourself, buying yourself nice things, dating and loving who you want, building a corporation or being the best damn housewife, you can be. For my men, your worth is not attached to what you can provide. As a man, you are a natural provider and you still deserved to be loved for who you are, not for what you give. Whatever you choose to hustle for, make sure you don't wrap your big "why" around caring for someone else when you need to look out for yourself, too. Love on others and take care of them only after you have taken care of yourself. If your hustle stops because you haven't taken care of yourself and your future, it will not only affect your family and friends, but also the "future" you who deserves your love, too.

Now that we have talked about some of the pitfalls we as hustlers need to avoid, let's talk about the lies society tries to place on us. Hustlers get a bad rap out here in the streets, but as a hustler, you know how to survive in good times or bad times. The point is for you to awaken your hustler spirit to survive in these times and for years to come.

Myths and Truths

Myth: Hustlers are bad Evil/Shady people.

Truth: Hustlers have the biggest hearts and visions.

When you hear the term hustler, most people picture a fast talking, slick man who smiles a lot to distract you from the venom they are about to strike you with. Although, there are some bad people in the world, most people are doing what they believe is right. People that are hustlers are hustling to feed their families or buy their mothers a home. Some may want to change their current circumstances or change the circumstances of the community they live in for the better. Whatever the hustler's reason, the truth is a true hustler has a heart to serve people and a big vision on how they will make it happen.

Another of my favorite real estate clients is Patrick Brown, also known in our city of Shreveport, Louisiana, as "Mr. I Got Cars for Sale". When you initially meet Mr. Brown, his apparent arrogance hits you in the face. He is very charismatic, making everyone laugh, and he is very confident in his responses to everything you say. Some may look at him as the slick used car salesman, but he has one of the biggest hearts and visions I have ever known. Initially, I brushed Mr. Brown off because I can say that I was intimidated by his confidence and crystal-clear vision. He had visions of owning a certain amount of property, owning his own car lot, and changing the community's thought process around ownership. In as little as six months, Mr. Brown did that and so much more. From the outside looking in people, would paint him as arrogant, but from the inside, his heart, vision, and work ethic will change the world.

Don't let the world put you in a box. Hustle hard, execute your vision, and change your world.

Myth: Money is evil and hustlers all worship money.

Truth: Money is good for the good it can do.

We have all heard the scripture in 1 Timothy 6:10: "For the love of money is the root of all kinds of evil." The rest of the verse reads: "And some people, craving money, have wandered from the true faith and pierced themselves with many sorrows." The verse doesn't say *money* is evil, it says the **love** of money is the cause (root) of ALL kinds of evil. To love something, you must have a deep interest or affection for that thing. When people love money, they want to hoard it, and have it all to themselves. When you hoard anything, it is

Hustle Under Pressure

for selfish security, not for the good it can do for you and those you love. For example, people are buying toilet paper by the truck load during this pandemic, not only because of what they need to use the toilet paper for. They are buying it to feel more secure, like a security blanket. They feel like they can't control anything else in the world, but they can control the amount of toilet paper they can have. The same happens when some people only pursue money to use it as a form of control. They use wealth for all kinds of evil of manipulation, oppression, and suffering. Most people on their hustle know this and they use money for the good it can be used for.

I love money for the great good it can be used for. Money is a form of energy that I attract to me and use for good. Poverty stricken people cannot not get to true clarity in life if their basic needs are not met. That makes them more prone to doing immortal, evil things to survive. In the poor, black community we have seen examples of good women and girls entertaining men just so they can pay rent or feed their kids; we have seen brilliant men commit low level crimes to survive; we have seen grandmother's take out pay day loans and are charged 300% interest to make ends meet; we have seen the elderly choose between food over heart medicine; we have seen hurt people, hurt people simply because everyone was angry that they were broke. That is evil.

Money is awesome. Money is your friend. Hustlers hustle because they know it is better to have the tool of money than the vice of idle time. To change your money mindset visit my uncle Rev. Ike (he is really not my uncle, but he is definitely one of my invisible mentors) https://youtu.be/wInbGxouz6Y .

Myth: Hustlers are opportunists.

Truth: Where others see problems, hustlers see opportunity!

I want to share a short story with you from https://www.topsarkarinaukri.in/seeing-opportunity-in-obstacles-a-motivational-story/

"Once there was a king who was curious but wealthy. He decided to test his fellow people to know who has a got a good attitude in life and who would spare some time for the country's progress. He placed a huge boulder right at the middle of the road and hid in a nearby place to see if anyone would try to move it off.

He saw some wealthy merchants and courtiers passing by the road. None of them made any attempt to move it off but simply walked away while some others blamed the king for not maintaining roads.

Later, a peasant came the way with a load of vegetables and saw the boulder. He sat his load

Hustle Under Pressure

down and tried to move the boulder away. After strenuous effort, he succeeded in moving it away. He saw a purse lying in the place of the boulder.

It contained many gold coins and a note from the king which read 'this is the reward for the person who moves the boulder away'."

Moral: It is quite common for people to run away from problems and obstacles. But this story clearly shows the importance of seeing an opportunity in every obstacle that might improve our condition. Invest some time to remove obstacles on your way and experience many unseen presences."

What boulders do you see in your home, life, community, or world? Instead of walking around them or ignoring them, find a way to move them and change your world!

Chapter 3: That's Law!

"I'm a real hustler so don't knock it, that's law
It's all about the re-up and the profit, that's law"
- Yo Gotti *Law*

"Things may come to those who wait, but only the things left by those who hustle."
– Abraham Lincoln

The Oxford dictionary defines hustle as "a force (someone) to move hurriedly or unceremoniously in a specified direction". The Oxford dictionary also defines a hustler as "an aggressively enterprising person, a go-getter". I deeply agree with both definitions. People know me as a hustler turned businesswoman, but ever since I could remember, I have been hurling in this direction. Sometimes I was so determined that I even scared myself. One time I flew to New York for one day by myself and stayed in a hotel where the bathroom was shared by everyone on that floor to buy knock off bags to resell them. I made $10,000 that summer off purse sells. I was determined to win because I knew the life I wanted to live, and I was determined to get it. Now I make enough money to support myself, my family, and extended family if needed. People see my current success in real estate and say, "You came out of nowhere!" or "You are lucky you found your niche!" Out loud, I say, "Thank you!", but in my head, I say, "Bullshit, I been out here!" I have done just about everything apart from selling my body or making others sell their bodies. There are a million other ways to make money legally that won't compromise your morals. To make money like the supreme hustlers we are, we have to stick to the laws.

A law of nature, like gravity or relativity, cannot be broken. Either you work with it or it will work against you. For example, if you jump out of a tree, you can believe with all your might that you will be able to fly. What will happen, though, is you will hit the ground hard and likely hurt yourself. It's the same with the laws of hustling. No matter how creative you are, what's law is law.

As with everything on this Earth that is seen and unseen, there are laws. What goes up must come down; for every action, there is an equal and opposite reaction. Now, if you choose to hustle, you must follow the laws. Of course, these laws are not all the "laws", but they are the foundational *hustler's* laws. To be a true go-getter, these laws must be engraved in your heart and followed.

Hustler Law 1: You Can't Get Something for Nothing

Every time I have tried to get something for nothing, I have regretted it. One time, I had a girl braid my hair when I was in high school. I decided not to pay her because it was her first time and I wanted to flex my bully muscles. Not only did my hair fall out in patches after that, I remember getting into an altercation at a club when I was by myself and guess who was right there looking at me struggle by myself. You got it - the same girl I didn't pay for doing my hair! Ouch!

Ralph Waldo Emerson wrote in his essay, *Compensation*, that each person is compensated in like manner for that which he or she has contributed. The Law of Compensation is basically this: you reap what you sow.

As a hustler never try to get something for nothing because you will receive **double** nothing in return.

Hustler Law 2: Do More Than is Expected

As I mentioned earlier in my story about local DJ legend, Mr. Hollyhood, BayBay, himself, he would blow the leaves out of his elderly neighbor's yard whenever he did his own yard and he would do it for free. He always gave his party-goers more than they expected. Another local party promoter I greatly respect is Sylvester Marshall. Mr. Marshall always goes above and beyond at the events he hosts. He doesn't call his gatherings "parties", he calls them "experiences", and that's exactly what they are. Your visual and audio senses are fully engaged with beautiful people, décor, food, and music. All his events make me feel like I have stepped inside a story book. What has impressed me the most about Mr. Marshall is his willingness to do more to make all his ventures come together.

In addition to being a party promoter, Mr. Marshall also owns a luxury vehicle transportation company. One year, I rented one of his Mercedes Sprinter vans for my best friend's birthday. Mr. Marshall's driver didn't show up that day, so Mr. Marshall drove all the way from New Orleans to drive me, my best friend, and another friend around all day. He was gracious and professional. Success will follow him because he could have said "I am the boss; I will not drive. People in Shreveport don't support my business enough, so I won't make the venue extravagant." Instead, he did more than was expected of him that day and I am sure he gets more than he has ever dreamed out of life.

When hustling, do more, not just to get back more. Do more because that is what will set you apart from the others.

Hustler Law 3: Respect the Game, but Play to Win

Whenever you play any sport or game, the game's organizers talk a lot about sportsmanship. The

Oxford dictionary defines sportsmanship as fair and generous behavior or treatment of others, especially in a sports contest. For hustlers it is a must that you respect the game and everyone in it. Even if you are working for a company, you must respect those in the company that are excelling at a high level, and still play to win. My friend, Jamila, is an excellent example of this. Whatever company she works for, she follows the same pattern every time. First, she studies the history of the company. She knows the mission, purpose, and how the company was started. Then she talks to the top agents at the company and asks them how they maximize their results. She also asks them what their biggest challenge is and if they could start over, where they would start. After she gathers all that information and puts her own spin on what needs to be done, she shoots straight to the top every time. I have never seen her go to any company and be mediocre. She is a genius that respects the game and plays to win.

How can you use a formula like Jamila's to respect the game and play to win?

Hustler Law 4: Don't Run Off on the Plug

I'm going to quote one of my favorite artist Jay-Z from his Nipsey Hussle Freestyle about not running off on the plug:

> How we gonna get in power if we kill the source?
> Y'all like to run off on the plug, so of course

> That ain't lit, that's a means to an end
> Me and my team was playing the plug ahead of plan
> Sometimes we was only making a $1000 a joint
> That ain't no money, but that ain't main point
> So those 92 bricks was only 92 thou
> So y'all can close your mouth, it ain't nothing for y'all to wild (Wow)

First let me define what "the plug" means. UrbanDictornary.com defines a plug as a person who has everything you need. In business, the plug is the distributor or even the CEO. So in referencing Jay Z's lyrics, what he is saying is that the person that has the work or the information don't be so short sighted and just try to take them for a gain today, when you can learn from them, use their product to get your gains up, and then use the knowledge and opportunity they have given you to execute your own plan.

In other words, Jay Z and his team had a plan to start their own company. They knew that even though they were only making $1000 per product from the distributor, they did their job, and the distributor trusted them enough to give the 92 units of product. They saved their $92,000 and started their own company, which is now worth billions! If they had cut out their distributors too early, they would have had only had thousands, and a bad reputation. Instead they stuck to their plan and now they have a legacy of billions. Do you get the point?

If someone is willing to trust you with products and information, do the right thing, honor the relationship, and build your reputation honorably. Then you must execute your plan.

Hustler Law 5: Know When to STFU! Listen More Talk Less

This should be law Number 1. Sometimes we talk too much when we need to listen. I am guilty of this because I want people to know how capable, smart, and funny I am. I am a realtor in Shreveport, Louisiana, and I am proud of my record, especially the one from my rookie year. I sold nearly $6 million in real estate and brought home $198,000. I was downright beaming with pride.

When I looked around my industry, I found out the great, talented, sweet, always-willing to-share-information top agent in our area, Tammi Montgomery, and her team has sold over $90 million in real estate! That means they brought home about $2.7 million! Glory! They donate to their favorite charities every month and are present in their family's lives. I quickly STFU and started listening. Anytime she is somewhere speaking I make a point to be there to soak in as much knowledge as possible. I ask her private questions. Whatever she says to do, I do my best to implement it. Everyone feels the need to be important. It is more important to listen than to speak. Just make sure you are listening to someone who is winning in the game and not standing on the side lines.

Hustler Law 6: Invest Back in the Re-up

To re-up means investing your time and money *back* into whatever product or service you are providing. If you cut hair, you need to invest in top of the line equipment and training. If you sell a product, buy more products and get coaching from those at the top in that business. If you sell real estate, get mastery coaching, and put money into advertising. If you work for a company, invest in additional training, and going to your local, regional, and national trade shows. Whatever it is that you do, invest in it so that you can provide the best to the customers you serve.

Hustler Law 7: Be the Face of Hustle

In our brains, we have something called the reticular activating system (RAS). The RAS is a bundle of nerves located at our brainstem that helps us focus on what we want and moves what we don't want out of the way. For example, if you say in your mind, *I need to buy a house,* everywhere you look and everything you hear after that will remind you of buying a house. It will show up on your Facebook feed, you will hear co-workers talking about it, you will see signs about purchasing a home, you will see it on TV. That is your RAS going to work! So, knowing that as a hustler, make use of everyone's RAS. Be the face of your hustle so when people think of the service you provide, they think of you.

If you are passionate about washing cars, post every day, at least three times a day about different cars you wash, how to get stains out of seats, how to keep your car clean between detailing, etc. Then when someone activates their RAS to get their car detailed, their RAS puts you front and center in their mind.

To learn how to be top-of-mind in your field, go listen to my homeboy (in my head), Gary Vee. He is a marketing genius. Check him out at [Top 2020 Marketing Strategies That Will Put You on the Map | RD Summit 2019](#).

Hustler Law 8: Put the next generation on game

Many business books say the same thing: every good leader has a successor, someone to carry the torch when you stop doing whatever it is you do. People have successors to carry on their vision, dream, and legacy. Some do it so that the youth will have a skill to survive. Whatever your reason is for passing on your knowledge, just make sure you do it. It is hard to explain the blessing that happens in your life when you pass on your legacy of knowledge. It is a hustle law because as a hustler, you need the support of a mentor and the energy of a student to carry on.

Hustle Under Pressure

Hustler Law 9: Stash back for a rainy day

This law is as important as breathing. What COVID-19 has shown us is that saving for hard times is not a choice, but a law. No matter how much you make, you must put back something for tough times. Some people put back 10% of their income. People like my husband put back 25% of their income. My mentor once said he lives off 50% of his income, which means he saves 50%. Whatever amount you are comfortable with, do that, because you absolutely cannot afford not to.

Hustler Law 10: Accountability

Some hustlers don't like to be checked on because they feel like that throws them off their game. I say every game has a good coach or partner. You need to be held accountable for your efforts to reach your goals and dreams so when you get tired, weary, or discouraged, you have an accountability partner to push you. Seek out a mentor in your desired field and let them help you stay focused.

Now that we know our core laws it is time to Go and Hustle!

Chapter 4: Go and Hustle!

"My entire life can be summed up in four words: I hustled. I conquered."
– Unknown

Before you dive into the next chapter full of ideas that will make your account fatter in these lean times, make sure you take heed of the pitfalls, myths, truths, and laws of hustling. We are in a crazy world now because of this virus. In all seriousness, some people don't know how they will make it, and will not bounce back from this devasting pandemic. COVID-19 has made us realize that we are not ready mentally, physically, spiritually, or financially. What happens after this will affect every generation to come for the next hundred years, at least.

How you react today will have implications on your great, great, great grandchildren. My heart is broken at the thought of how the gap between the "haves" and "have nots" went from the size of a valley to the size of an ocean overnight. My writing this book had little to do with me making money and more to do with the world my daughter will have to live in after this is over. To bring it all the way down, I love my daughter, Leeyah, so much and to think she will live in world where depression is rampant because of the aftereffects of isolation and overwhelming debt makes me weep uncontrollably.

My anxiety over the thought of Leeyah's beautiful, funny light being dimmed because of the potential viciousness of people who are weighed down by debt and disconnectedness, makes my heart race. I screamed out, "God what can I do to help change the world for my dear Leeyah?" His answer was to *teach people how to hustle like you have done your whole life. Teach people how I allowed you not to have the comfort of an Earthly father to help you with your needs. Teach people the passion I gave you to buy your mom two homes. Show people the money moves I gave you to help your husband pay off a $40k vehicle and $20k of debt in nine months. Teach people to survive by any means necessary that does not comprise their soul or morals. Teach people how I have kept you through dark times and never left you lonely because I live in you like I live in them.*

To God I said yes because I'll be damned if I don't live more from this day forward and if I don't do everything in my power to change the world for my city, my family, my state, my world, and most of all, for my Leeyah. Take this guide and go hustle for your life and for the lives attached to yours. I love y'all. Hustle hard!

XOXO

Marian

Chapter 5: 111 Ways

Considering our current times, having one source of income is a thing of the past. Experts have always stated that having at least five streams of income is best. Starting today, implement a few of the strategies below to help you with your financial goals of freedom from debt , a healthy savings account, a big purchase, or whatever your goal maybe. Disclaimer: I have not done all the ventures listed below so please do your due diligence on the companies mentioned before participating in their programs. A lot of these ideas come from one of my favorite sites https://www.sidehustlenation.com/ideas/. Others come from hustles I have done or desire to do soon.

Ready? Let's Go!

1. **Arise.com**

Arise is a customer experience innovator that shatters obstacles that impede the customer care industry. The Arise Platform delivers radical flexibility and on-demand burst-capacity at scale.

Basically, you can start your own call center from the comfort of your home. You can do it yourself or have other people working for you. You can be a call center operator for companies that do everything from fitness and wellness to cruises! Make your own schedule and take advantage of the low start-up cost opportunity.

2. Parish or city government contracting

Did you know you can get paid to provide things like toilet paper to your city? Yes, really toilet paper! I had a friend who had her own L.L.C. She bid on a project through the City of Shreveport to provide Government Plaza's toilet paper supply. I don't remember the exact figure, but all she did was submit a bid to provide the toilet paper, let's say at $2.00 a roll, to the City. She won the bid. She went and purchase rolls for $0.50 each and dropped them off every month at the Government Plaza building. She made $1.50 per roll. Let's say she delivered 5000 rolls over the course of a year. That means she made $7500 in a year just by dropping off toilet paper!!

The city has RFPs (request for proposals) for everything from toilet paper to special trainings to work boot orders. For the City of Shreveport you can go to https://www.shreveportla.gov/1495/Solicitations or to https://prod.bidsync.com/ for bid opportunities.

3. State government contracting

Just as city governments do, state governments also have different projects that individuals or businesses can bid on. You say you don't have experience doing some of the services or perhaps you don't have the items requested? No worries, just bring the experienced partners to the table and get paid for it!

That's a whole different topic for another day. For the State of Louisiana RFPs visit https://wwwcfprd.doa.louisiana.gov/osp/lapac/srchopen.cfm

4. Federal government contracting

Just like city and state governments, the feds are looking for individuals and companies that can provide services from driving to picking up trash to providing security details. For more information of Federal RFPs go to https://beta.sam.gov/.

5. Sell stuff on eBay and/or Craigslist

We all have too much stuff and the truth is, one person's trash is another person's treasure. Look around your home and office and see what you can sell. Go to garage sales and buy cheap then sell higher. Visit https://www.ebay.com/ or https://shreveport.craigslist.org/ or https://craigslist.org/ for your city.

6. Sell stuff on Decluttr

Scan the barcodes on old books and CDs and other electronics, and know what Decluttr will pay you instantly! They will make a direct deposit into your account after the items are received. I think this is kind of neat because you can go to a garage sale or Goodwill, scan stuff, and see if it's worth buying! Visit https://www.decluttr.com/

7. Drive for Uber or Lyft

Like to drive and meet new people? Well, taxi them around and get paid! This is completely flexible and can be done on your own time! In big cities you can make a good living. Visit https://www.uber.com/ or https://www.lyft.com/ for more information.

8. Deliver food through Waitr

Deliver food from local restaurants to local residents and make extra cash. Waitr let's your work around your own schedule. Visit https://waitrapp.com/

9. Airbnb

Have an extra room or even an extra home? Rent it out for money! No matter what kind of home or room you share, Airbnb makes it simple and secure to host travelers. You're in full control of its availability, prices, house rules, and how you interact with guests. Visit https://www.airbnb.com/

10. Justanswer.com

Are you an expert in a certain field? Get paid to answer questions from the general public! Just Answer provides a platform that connects experts like you with the public, online or via phone. Go to https://www.justanswer.com/ for more information.

11. Fiverr

According to their website, Fiverr's mission is to change how the world works together. Fiverr connects businesses with freelancers offering digital services in 250+ categories. Visit https://www.fiverr.com/ for more information.

12. Amazon Mechanical Turk

Amazon Mechanical Turk (MTurk) is a crowdsourcing marketplace that makes it easier for individuals and businesses to outsource their processes and jobs to a distributed workforce who can perform these tasks virtually. You can do tasks like research development, data entry, and survey participation from the comfort of your own home. Visit https://www.mturk.com/.

13. Amazon online store

Many people get products from sites like Alibaba and sell them to customers of their own through Amazon digital storefronts. Amazon is customer-centric and entrepreneur friendly. They have even produced this eBook to help you start your Amazon online store https://m.media-amazon.com/images/G/01/sell/guides/Beginners-Guide-to-Selling-on-Amazon.pdf?ld=NSGoogle. Imagine buying 100 units of a product for $0.50 and then selling it for $5.00 a piece! That means your $50 investment just turned it $500! Visit https://sell.amazon.com/sell.html?ref_=asus_soa_rd& for more information.

14. Online tutoring via Zoom or Skype

Now that social distancing is a thing and kids are home from school, virtual tutoring is a must! Speaking for myself, I will find a way for someone to engage my daughter in learning while I work from home. Tutors should set up Zoom or Skype accounts and market their services via Facebook and Instagram. Take payments via CashApp, Zelle, or PayPal. In these times, some teachers will probably make more than they normally would in a traditional classroom setting since now they can reach students all over the United States and world! Visit https://zoom.us/ or https://www.skype.com/en/.

15. Federal grant reviewer

One of my favorite side hustles was reviewing federal grants! Back when I did them in 2007 and 2008, they would fly me to DC or Maryland, put me and about 100 other people up in a fancy hotel, feed us well, and pay us about $2000 a week to read and review grants! Good times! Now I believe they do everything virtually. Either way, check it out if you love to read and have a good understanding of contracts and rubric criteria. Visit https://www.acf.hhs.gov/sites/default/files/assets/acf_grant_reviewer_english.pdf for grant review opportunities through the Administration on Children and Family services.

16. Create online courses
Udemy's website wants you to create an online video course and earn money by teaching it to people around the world. Earn money every time a student purchases your course. Get paid monthly through PayPal or Payoneer, it's your choice. Help people learn new skills, advance their careers, and explore their hobbies by sharing your knowledge. Visit https://www.udemy.com/teaching/.

17. Create sales funnels
I don't know exactly what this is, but it seems dope af! The videos on Click Funnel's website seems to describe getting global leads for your product or business through a sales funnel for people already looking for your product. I am excited to use it for this ebook! Visit https://www.clickfunnels.com/

18. Publish eBook
Have a book that you need to get out to the world? You can do it easily without having to go the traditional publishing route! What a time to be alive! Visit https://kdp.amazon.com/en_US/ or https://www.createspace.com/ for more information.

19. Publish an audiobook

Amazon is really the G.O.A.T. out here in these streets! They will help you to not only publish your eBook or printed book, they will also assist in creating an your audio version of your book! Visit https://www.amazon.com/gp/education-publishing/Audiobooks for more information.

20. Become a personal chef

Do you love to cook, and you *know* your meals are restaurant quality or better? Go list your services on HireAChief. Individuals or companies look for talented personal chefs for private events. Why not be their personal chef? Visit https://www.hireachef.com/ for more information.

21. Mystery shopping

I did this for a while in my 20s and I made decent money. I have read articles about people who make a good living by mystery shopping. They basically eat for free because they only eat when they get paid for it. You can also mystery shop hotels, gas stations, and many other places. Here are a few mystery shopping companies you should check out according to thepennyhoarder.com.

> https://apply.bestmark.com/?r=FL7420
> https://www.sinclaircustomermetrics.com/index.cfm

https://www.marketforce.com/become-a-mystery-shopper
https://www.intelli-shop.com/shoppers

22. Walk dogs

Do you like dogs and the outdoors? You would be the perfect dog walker! Owners get busy and they don't want their fur babies cooped up in the house all day. Some dog walkers make $1000 per month or more! OMG! If you see me out here walking dogs, mind your business. For dog walking opportunities visit:

https://www.rover.com/dog-walking-jobs/
https://petsitter.com/dog-walking-jobs
https://www.indeed.com/q-Walking-Dog-jobs.html
https://wagwalking.com/

23. Mobile dog groomer

The fur babies need pampering, too! Marry your love for pets and good grooming to open a mobile dog grooming company. The linked article says you will need $10k to start, but after reading it, I know you can find creative ways to start your business with a lot less money and still provide superior quality. Read this article and go get started https://www.entrepreneur.com/businessideas/mobile-pet-grooming.

24. Babysit/nanny service

Do you like kids and feel you are extra nurturing? Consider becoming a babysitter or nanny. In the State of Louisiana, you can care for up to six children and be considered a home daycare service receiving childcare assistance. Visit https://www.louisianabelieves.com/docs/default-source/early-childhood/provider-types.pdf?sfvrsn=2 for more information regarding Louisiana's laws or visit your states department of education website for more information. You can also keep it small and just care for a few kids by finding jobs at https://care.com or https://www.sittercity.com/

25. Clean homes

Of course, as is the case with most companies like the ones mentioned above, it is advised that you establish a legal business entity. Please consult with an attorney for specific state laws. In most states, if you are conducting a cleaning business, bond insurance may be required. Either way, if it's for the general public, friend, or relative, cleaning people's homes or apartments is a great way to earn extra cash. Check out platforms like HouseKeeper.com to get started.

26. Focus Groups

Participate in paid focus groups, test new products, taste new snacks and beverages, watch new TV shows, take online surveys, and more! Check out https://www.focusgroup.com/ for more information.

27. Garage sale
This tried and true activity has been around for years. Although you could post your stuff online and sell it, there is nothing like the human interaction of buying stuff and haggling in person. You can do it solo or get a group of friends together to hold a larger sale. It is a great way to make some extra cash. Check out this guide on garage sale pricing https://www.thespruce.com/dos-and-donts-of-yard-sale-pricing-1313857.

28. YouTube Channel/ Podcast
There are 6-year-old kids out there who are making money moves on YouTube, so why can't you? There are successful podcasts for everything under the sun. I see people on social media that are hilarious or super knowledgeable on subjects that parlay their content to make money. Social content can reach all around the world. Today, social media is literally keeping us all sane. You can monetize this by getting more business and affiliated marketing. My homeboy (in my head), Gary Vee, let's you know how important this platform is https://youtu.be/u4FXTWN4tV4.

29. Upwork
Upwork connects businesses of all sizes to freelancers, independent professionals, and agencies

for all their hiring needs. Flex your talent skills. Visit https://www.upwork.com/.

30. Be a Personal Shopper

Sometimes life gets busy and people need a little extra help shopping. If you are good at picking groceries (trust me it's a skill) or even choosing clothes, become a personal shopper. Go on platforms like https://www.thumbtack.com/ to post your services.

31. Odd jobs expert

In the Black community, we all have "that" friend or uncle or dad who does odd jobs. It is not an official job title or gender specific, however, in 2020, our "odd jobs expert" can expand his or her network to do any number of jobs throughout the community. To find out job task go to platforms like https://www.taskrabbit.com/.

32. Artsy/Crafty Peeps

If you make handcrafted, unique pieces, Esty is the place for you. Esty has created a web-based store for creatives to sell their goods to people around the world. For more information visit https://www.etsy.com/?ref=lgo.

33. Personal fitness trainer

If you are in love with fitness, help others reach their weight loss goals by becoming a personal trainer. If you get certified to help whip people in shape, that's even better, but it's not required. You can have classes in person or online. You can even have personal sessions. Read this article on how to help you become a personal fitness trainer https://www.acefitness.org/fitness-certifications/personal-trainer-certification/how-to-become-a-personal-trainer.aspx.

34. Music Lessons

Just like tutoring online or in-person, you can give music or singing lessons in the same way. If you can teach people how to play an instrument or sing, set up Zoom or Skype accounts, and market your services via Facebook and Instagram. Take payments via CashApp, Zelle, or PayPal. Visit https://zoom.us/ or https://www.skype.com/en/.

35. Affiliate marketing

One of my very favorite ways to make money is through affiliate marketing! Basically, you create a following for yourself in any field you are passionate about, then you get brands to pay you to advertise their product! For a more in-depth conversation on how to make affiliate marketing opportunities work for you, check out this coaching video from Grant Cardone https://youtu.be/BO4u8bxXeZE.

36. Sell your hair
The hair market is a billion-dollar industry! Your long hair can put money in your pocket if you don't mind parting with it. *Wherever you are in the world, if your hair is over 6 inches, you can sell it on HairSellon!* HairSellon is the biggest international marketplace for buying and selling hair. They walk you through the entire process with the aim of an easy and fair experience for everyone. Visit https://hairsellon.com/.

37. Be a house sitter
There is a whole segment of the population that travels domestically and abroad for work or personal reasons and needs someone to get keep their homes. Why not you? Water the plants, do some light cleaning, check the mail, feed the fish, or snake. Check out https://housesitter.com/house-sitter-jobs if you want to make extra money being a house sitter.

38. Driver instructor
Do you love to drive and have nerves of steel? Become a driving instructor! Each state has its own requirements for this position so check with your state. Here in Louisiana, Driver's Education classes can range from $500-$700 per person! Check the DMV.gov for your state.

39. Virtual Assistant

Professionals are consistently looking for administrative type help online. From data entry to making phone calls. VAs can make up $60k a year from home! Check out this article to learn more https://gatheringdreams.com/how-to-become-a-virtual-assistant/.

40. Create an app

Do you have an app idea that you *know* will make big money? You can get someone to build it for you on sites like Elance or you get build it yourself. Check out this article on building your money-making app: https://buildfire.com/how-to-create-a-mobile-app/.

41. Teach English online

Teach English as a second language and make up to $22 per hour on your own schedule. Visit https://www.vipkid.com/teach for more information.

42. Get paid to interview

Respondent is a cool service that facilitates those interviews that take place both in-person and online. You can totally do this from home, just look for the ones that say "remote". Visit https://app.respondent.io/respondents/v2/signup?r=nickloper-17ef7e74a1be for more information.

43. Online survey completion

These won't make you rich but can be an easy way to supplement your income. Besides you can do them in your downtime (waiting in line, watching TV, etc.).

- Swagbucks – mega-popular survey platform with a free $10 bonus and the opportunity to earn up to $35 a survey.
- **Springboard America** – offers higher payouts than many other survey sites but requires a $50 minimum to cash out.
- **Survey Junkie** – popular online survey site with more than 3 million members.
- **Vindale Research** – earn up to $50 per survey.
- **Prize Rebel** – earn $10-12 an hour doing surveys or completing other tasks. Just avoid the low-paying ones.
- InboxDollars (free $5 bonus)
- **Opinion Outpost** – cash out at just $5 via PayPal or Amazon gift cards.

44. Rent Your Car for Profit

Rent out your car on turo.com or getaround.com. We used to call it a "rent-a-rock" in the hood, but look at colonization! Won't He Do It! Visit https://turo.com/ **or** https://www.getaround.com/.

45. Blogging

Blogging is another content sharing medium that can get you big bucks if you market it just right.

Check out this article on making money as a blogger: https://www.wpbeginner.com/beginners-guide/make-money-online/.

46. Notary

Get paid to officially witness documents. Each state has different requirements in becoming a notary. This article will let you know how to get started https://www.nationalnotary.org/knowledge-center/about-notaries/how-to-become-a-notary-public.

47. Private labeling

In this side hustle, you identify hot-selling products and bring your own to market for competition with others. There's an art and science to this, including negotiating with suppliers (often overseas), but in this episode of The Side Hustle Show, 7-figure Amazon seller, Greg Mercer, shared his top three tips Amazon FBA product sourcing guidelines and tips.

48. Baking

Do you have a talent for baking? Make money sharing those sweet treats. Read this article on how to get started https://www.thepennyhoarder.com/make-money/side-gigs/selling-baked-goods-from-home/.

49. Get paid to lose weight

My prayers have been answered! I can get paid to lose weight. If you are competitive, Healthy Wage is for you. It helps you organize weight loss challenges where you can win money if you lose big. Check out https://www.healthywage.com/.

50. Become an Adjunct Professor
This is a bucket list item for me. I love teaching adults and it seems like it would be interesting. Each college or institution has its own requirements for becoming an adjunct professor. Reach out to local colleges in your area and online colleges.

51. Tax prep
I have a client who makes big business out of doing taxes and helping others set up tax prep companies. She works hard from December through April and virtually has the rest of the year off. If you are interested in starting your own tax prep company, reach out to Dequita at 299 Tax prep to start your tax prep business https://form.jotform.com/93075847293165.

52. Raw land flipping
One of my favorite sites is Side Hustle Nation and recently, they did a segment on how to flip raw land for profit. Go check it out https://www.sidehustlenation.com/land-flipping/

53. Book flipping
If you are like me, you have lots of books just laying around. I love my books, but there are some I can let go of. I love selling my books on Book Scouter. I just scan the barcode with my phone or type in the title and ship them to Book Scouter and

get money deposited into my account. HustleTip: Scan books at garage sales or book sales and see if they are worth purchasing for an easy flip. Check out https://bookscouter.com/

54. Sperm Donor

Fellas, if you don't mind sharing your seeds with the world then sperm donation is for you. Each state and city has local laws and places associated with donating your sperm. Check out this article to get you started https://www.mayoclinic.org/tests-procedures/sperm-donation/about/pac-20395032. You could pocket an extra $200 per donation.

55. Egg Donor

Ladies, if you don't mind sharing your seeds with the world then egg donation is for you. Each state and city have local laws and places associated with donating your eggs. Unlike sperm donation, you can get $35,000-$50,000 per egg. Check out this article https://www.medicalnewstoday.com/articles/314750.

56. Blood Donor

Selling blood (i.e. your plasma) is good for your heart and pocket. Check out this article on the heart benefits of donating blood https://www.oneblood.org/media/blog/donor/how-donating-blood-impacts-your-heart.stml and the money benefits https://wallethacks.com/how-to-donate-plasma/.

57. Sell t-shirts

Do have a love of making t-shirts? You can sell them in your local market and on sites like https://teespring.com/signup.

58. Referee
Local schools and recreational centers pay people to referee games. You can make a little extra cash while watching your favorite sports. Check out this article on how to get started https://www.indeed.com/career-advice/pay-salary/how-much-do-referees-get-paid.

59. Pool cleaning
Make some extra cash cleaning pools. Start here to learn more https://www.thebalancesmb.com/small-business-ideas-pool-cleaning-service-4045992.

60. Lawn service
Make yards pretty again and make your pockets fat. Here is an article that will help guide you through getting started https://www.yourgreenpal.com/blog/how-to-start-a-lawn-care-business.

61. Pest Control
If you are not scared of the creepy, crawly things, consider starting a pest control company. Pest control can get you $100-$1000 per job. Check out this article on how to get started: https://www.serviceautopilot.com/10-steps-to-starting-your-own-pest-control-business/.

62. Alterations
Let your love for sewing put money in your pocket. Market your services online and watch the opportunities roll in. Watch this video by Angela Wolf to get started https://youtu.be/Wskybo0c6-g.

63. Brand Ambassador
I have always thought this was a cool job. When I was in college, I remember I wanted to be a Remy Martin girl. These beautiful ladies were picked to represent Remy Martin as brand ambassadors. Today you can be a brand ambassador on social media for money and/or free products. For more information check out Tyra The Creative on How to be a Brand Ambassador https://youtu.be/RH_rtaMLP9c

64. Car flipping
Have a talent for fixing up cars? Check out this Side Hustle Nation article on flipping cars https://www.sidehustlenation.com/car-flipping/.

65. Vending machines
This something I plan on doing with my daughter very soon. I have always wanted to own vending machines. Check out *Earn Your Leisure*, a YouTube video that shows an interview with the vending machine king, **Kashief Edwards** https://youtu.be/MyPyZhF1xEk ! I'm super motivated by him!

66. Carpet cleaning

Clean carpets for a profit. Here is an article that will help you get started https://www.fundera.com/blog/how-to-start-a-carpet-cleaning-business

67. Computer tutoring
Some people have challenges with technology. One of my favorite things to do when I worked at the local library was to teach elderly people how to work their devices. Of course, we didn't charge them, but that would be a good business. Check with the local college to teach continuing education classes on this. Today more than ever, people need to know how to utilize technology to stay connected.

68. Facebook and Instagram business profile creations
This is a challenge for me, and I will pay someone to setup all my platforms so I can streamline my companies. If you have a talent for this, make it a business.

69. Get Paid to go out on dates
In real life, this is a thing! You can get paid to go out on dates! Who said you can't make money because being pretty? If you are interested, check out https://www.whatsyourprice.com/ today!

70. Doula services

This is a bucket list item for me, and it can be a money-maker for you today. Help a mother bring life into the world with your calming demeanor and make extra cash while doing it. Check out https://www.dona.org/become-a-doula/birth-doula-certification/ for more information.

71. Estate sales services

As a real estate agent, I come across properties all the time that have years of accumulated stuff that needs to be sold. Estate sales companies come in and sell the stuff for the client, for a fee and sometimes a cut of the profit. Check out https://estatesales.org/university/start-an-estate-sale-company for steps on how to start.

72. DJ

Have dreams of rocking the crowd? Become a DJ. Here is a guide to get you started https://www.wirerealm.com/info/how-to-become-a-dj.

73. Party Host/Hostess

Your outgoing, charismatic personality can get you extra cash as a party host. Keep people engaged and the party going. Check out this article to get started **https://livingsimplyfabulous.com/make-money-hosting-parties/.**

74. Retail auditing

Field Agent is your on-demand platform for retail audits, mystery shops, market research, digital product demonstrations, and online ratings and reviews. Get paid per completed task. Go to <ins>https://www.fieldagent.net/</ins> for more information.

75. Human billboard
We laugh at the Liberty Tax guy dancing on the corner, however, with further research I see he might be on to something. According to ziprecruiter.com, human billboards make an average of about $50k per year!! For more information on how to become a human billboard, check out this article <ins>https://www.thepennyhoarder.com/make-money/side-gigs/nomad-human-billboard/</ins>.

76. Junk hauling/clean outs
Some people abandon their homes and apartments and leave all their stuff behind. Get paid to clean out what they left behind. Market to apartment complexes, realtors, and property managers. Hustle Tip: Start a thrift store with what is left behind or put it on eBay. You're welcome!

77. Rent your baby stuff
Have old baby stuff? Get money by renting it out. In response to COVID-19, BabyQuip.com **has you covered. Go check out** BabyQuip.com **for more information.**

78. Product Licensing

next venture I will tackle is product licensing. After reading Stephen Key's book *One Simple Idea,* I have been fascinated with licensing out one of my many inventions. If you have an idea or invention you want to get to market without having to produce a prototype, check out https://www.inventright.com/.

79. Be a consultant
Are you an expert of at anything? Great! You can be a consultant. Consultants do a range of things and get paid a range of money. I have a friend who is a consultant and she simply connects one professional to another professional and gets a cut in between. Check out this article to get you started https://blog.hubspot.com/sales/how-to-become-a-consultant.

80. Get paid to be a friend
That's right get paid to be friendly—no funny business, just friends. Just do your due diligence before you participate. Check out https://rentafriend.com/index/ for more information.

81. Snuggle for money
Get paid to lay around and provide social interaction. Check out https://snugglebuddies.com/ for more information.

82. Get paid to have a Sugar Daddy
Yes, you read it right. If you want to be a kept woman, this site states that Sugar Babies are beautiful women seeking arrangements and

relationships with wealthy and successful men. For more information https://sugarbabies.co/m

83. Stock Photos
Like taking pictures? Sell them as stock photos that can be used for projects around the world. Here is an article to get you started https://www.pixpa.com/blog/sell-stock-photos.

84. Stock Music
Compose music pieces that can be used on commercials or online or wherever. Check out this article to get you started **https://www.sidehustlenation.com/music-licensing/.**

85. Travel Agent
After this COVID-19 stuff is over, travel will be at an all-time high! I have a date with the pyramids myself. My travel agent, Erica Ledet, is a director with PlanNet Marketing. Reach out to her to become a travel agent from home. Visit her website at
https://PlanNetMarketing.com/prettyflydestinations

86. Get paid to wrap your vehicle
Get paid hundreds of dollars per month to drive around and advertise for brands. Visit https://www.wrapify.com/ to get started.

87. Voiceover

Make money use your voice. Watch Carrie on my favorite podcast, His and Her Money Show. to learn how to get started https://youtu.be/TZw7rWqJ4Do.

88. Professional Organizer

Where they at, though? I need this person in my life right now! I am clean, but I love to see things organized. If you are super organized and everything you do looks like it comes straight off of Pinterest, become a professional organizer. Check out this article to get you started https://crowdworknews.com/become-professional-organizer/.

89. Real estate house flipper

My husband and I have flipped a few homes and we love the process. To see something go from ugly and nasty to beautiful and fresh is amazing. The profit is amazing, too! We have made from $25k to $40k per flip! You can, too. I love Biggerpockets.com. Check out this article on how to flip properties with no money out of pocket https://www.biggerpockets.com/blog/2012-09-08-flip-houses-with-no-money.

90. Real Estate Wholesaler

I was a real estate wholesaler before I became a realtor. I found motivated sellers, hooked them up with willing buyers, and I made a cut in between. Best thing is I did it with very little money - I'm talking like $50. On my first wholesale deal, I made $4000! Check out this article at BiggerPockets.com

to learn about wholesaling
https://www.biggerpockets.com/blog/wholesaling-60-day-guide.

91. Landlord

There are tons of ways to become a landlord with little to no money out of pocket. One of my real estate mentors, Louis Fourquet, says it best, "The name of the game is to control the property, not necessarily own it." Check out this article on how to get started with getting rental property https://www.biggerpockets.com/blog/rental-property-investing-101.

92. Primerica

Primerica Financial Marketing has been around for a while and even though it is mult-level marketing, the life insurance, investments, securities, prepaid legal, home/auto insurance, and debt reduction plans, are things that are needed by everyone. If you are interested in signing up, reach out to my friend, Terrance Neal, at terranceneal@primerica.com.

93. Thrive

THRIVE Experience is a premium lifestyle system that helps you experience peak physical and mental levels, according to their website. Their products are all-natural and I love the Iaso tea with Hemp and the energy pills. You can earn up to $20 per product sold. Reach out to my friend Thedora Coleman to start with Thrive today https://linktr.ee/thecolemancrew.

94. Property preservation
My dear husband purchased a used truck for me when I was doing property preservation. Man, his support for me is dope! Anyway, I digress. Mortgage companies need preservation companies to check if homes are vacated and if they are, property preservation companies are hired for a range of things from taking pictures to mowing the lawn to changing locks. To learn how to start your property preservation business, check out https://www.vrmco.com/news/how-to-grow-your-property-preservation-business-in-2020/.

95. Nelson television ratings
Nielsen is a market research company that studies the behaviors of consumers for companies, both large and small. I was a Nielsen Television Ratings Membership Representative for two years and I loved it. I worked from home, but I traveled a lot with the company. They gave me a company car, laptop, and printer. You could work for the company or just participate as one of their panelists. Visit https://www.nielsen.com/us/en/contact-us/panels/ for more information.

96. Truck driver
Because of this COVID-19 crisis, there is a shortage on drivers to deliver goods, but even before this pandemic, drivers were essential to our economy. Each state has requirements for drivers, so to get

you started, check out this article https://www.learnhowtobecome.org/truck-driver/. Drivers can make from $40k-$100k+ a year.

97. Cash back on shopping
Earn cash back when you do your general shopping and grocery shopping using apps like Ibotta. Visit **https://home.ibotta.com/ for more information.**

98. Property management
Manage rental properties for landlords/property owners for a percentage of the rent collected per month. To find out how to get started, check out this article **https://money.howstuffworks.com/how-to-start-property-management-company.htm.**

99. Independent cable contractor
Installing cable and broadband internet as an independent cable contractor is a very lucrative business. I have a friend who earns on average $20K per month. To get started, check out this article on how to get started with DirecTV **https://smallbusiness.chron.com/become-directv-contract-company-30949.html.**

100. Restore bicycles
My brother, Andy, used to do this when we were younger, and he wanted a new bike. My mom couldn't afford to get him one, so he took old bicycle parts, put them together, painted them, and he had a new bike. Now that we are restricted from going places, this is a trend that will be profitable for the maker. Read this article to motivate you to

get started **https://onemorecupof-coffee.com/make-money-flipping-bicycles/.**

101. Alarm system sales
I have a client who makes over six-figures selling alarm systems. Alarm systems! Check out this YouTube video on selling for different alarm system companies https://youtu.be/HlRh9PCasD4.

102. Utilities sales
In some states, there are multiple utility providers for water, sewage, and electricity. Here in Louisiana, we don't have many options, but our neighbors in Texas do. Reach out to local utility companies to see if they have a door-to-door vendor program for you to sell utilities. Check out https://acn.com/us-en/opportunity. Their system is set up so you can start your home based business easily.

103. Pharmaceuticals/ Medical Sales Representative
Be a legal drug dealer and make a good living doing it. Check out this YouTube video to get started https://youtu.be/qdi4dPv1Gus.

104. Merchandisers (various magazine, Hallmark, cigarette makers, etc.)
You can be a merchandiser for all sorts of things, for example, cigarettes, greeting cards, magazines, chips, liquor, and beer. Check out this article on top 10 merchandiser positions you can work from home **https://workathomemomrevolution.com/field-**

merchandising/10-companies-that-hire-home-based-field-merchandisers/.

105. Shopify

Set up an online store, quick and easy, with Shopify. Check out this article so you can learn to start your business today **https://www.shopify.com/blog/how-to-start-a-business.**

106. Video Editing

People shoot videos all the time, but they don't always know how to edit them. This is great for everyone from families, to small companies, and large companies. Check out this video to help you get started https://youtu.be/iw-7YYupOY4.

107. Realtor

Well, duh! Lol! You can make an average of $2000 extra per month with one sale. I love real estate and I could write another book on real estate sales, but trust me this business is super dope and super worth it. The first thing to do is take your real estate class online or in person. I took my class online and here is a link if you are interested in it. Just select whichever state you are in to get started http://trk.realestateexpress.com/?a=13608&c=1054&p=r&s1=. After that, you will take the national and state exams. For exam help, check out *Prep Agent* on YouTube https://www.youtube.com/user/PrepAgent.

108. Help people move

It is like the Uber of moving services. Join Dolly and use your truck, trailer, or just your hands to get paid working whenever you choose to. Check out https://dolly.com/helpers/ for more information.

109. Build a subscription box business.
Whether you love picking the perfect beauty products or have a knack for putting together the best snack boxes, you can create and sell your own custom subscription boxes online using a site like CrateJoy for some extra income. Visit **https://www.cratejoy.com/**.

110. Elderly services
Elderly services are passion businesses and they provide big money. Check out these 10 elderly service businesses that will fuel your passion to help and finance your greatest life at **https://www.entrepreneur.com/article/334861.**

111. Sell your old clothes
Do you have a lot of old clothes? Sell them online to companies like ThredUp. Thredup states that they are the world's largest online secondhand shopping destination with thousands of like-new styles from your favorite brands at up to 90% off estimated retail. They make sure every single one of the 15K new arrivals they add to their site every day is 100% authentic and in such good shape, anyone could mistake them for new. Visit their site today at https://www.thredup.com/.

This list can go on and on! There is opportunity all around us. I hope this list and the other information in this guide helps you along the road to your financial goals.

About the Author

Marian Claville Burks is a licensed realtor at what she believes is the best real estate brokerage organization in the world, Keller Williams Realty NWLA in Shreveport, Louisiana. There, she heads up The Marian Home Group. She is the proud mother of Leeyah, and the loving, supportive wife of Ledell. She is a community activist on a mission to empower, encourage, educate, and motivate people to create generational wealth. She strives to help others become financially independent, grow companies and business of excellence, and to realize their full potential in life. She helps her clients make wise wealth-related decisions in the areas of real estate and business creation.

Let's Connect!

Connect with Marian and follow the hustle on the following platforms:

https://www.instagram.com/hustleunderpressure/

https://www.facebook.com/Hustle-Under-Pressure-Awaken-the-Hustle-in-You-to-Survive-Uncertain-Times-113204750330651/settings/?tab=instagram_management&ref=page_edit

https://twitter.com/PressureHustle

hustleunderpressure.com

Made in the USA
Middletown, DE
24 July 2020